This year can be more beautiful

than the last, starting now. The 365 upbeat suggestions in these pages present the opportunity to make the world a little better every day of the year. The ideas may be simple (*Give a sincere compliment*), heartwarming (*Cuddle a newborn*), or unexpected (*Be nice to phone solicitors*). They may be encouraging Bible verses (*Practice real love*, 1 John 3:18) or inspiring quotes (*Notice God everywhere*, Elizabeth Dreyer).

Let this journal inspire small kindnesses, big accomplishments, and journaling moments. Use the lines on each dated page to reflect on the day's prompt, record events and plans, or write down your prayers. Start any time, and continue until you've filled the whole year with thoughtful acts.

Each day holds the chance to do something beautiful for others—or yourself. And as you intentionally embrace each opportunity, you'll find yourself doing something beautiful for God.

January 1

Celebrate the start of each new day with God.

WENDY MOORE

....
....
....
....
....
....

January 2

Create
opportunities
by seeing the possibilities and having
the persistence to act upon them.

....

....

....

....

....

January 3

Want to
Give of
yourself

and don't know where to start?
Do a Google search with the word "volunteer"
and your profession.
Include a city or state to narrow your search.

....

....

....

....

....

....

January 4

Go out in joy and be led forth in peace.

ISAIAH 55:12 NIV

....

....

....

....

....

....

January 5

Read a good book.
Then give it away.

....
....
....
....
....
....

January 6

Print photos for grandparents

who may not be comfortable
with the latest technology.

....

....

....

....

....

....

January 7

Be considerate.

Pull up to the last gas pump
so that others can
access available pumps.

January 8

Sing to GOD a brand~new song,

sing his praises all over the world!

ISAIAH 42:10 MSG

....

....

....

....

....

January 9

Hug
someone
who
needs one.
(That's just about everyone.)

....

....

....

....

....

....

Dance like there's nobody watching.

WILLIAM W. PURKEY

January 11

With a checkerboard under
your arm, walk over and

Turn off
the TV.

Announce, "It's time for a
checkers tournament."

....

....

....

....

....

January 12

Seek,
and
you will
find.

LUKE 11:9 NKJV

....

....

....

....

....

....

Sit somewhere new at church.

Make new friends.

Get a new perspective.

....

....

....

....

....

....

January 14

Don't win an argument
but lose a friend.

Always
keep the
door open
for another healthy debate.

....
....
....
....
....
....

January 15

Make this a special day for someone who needs a lift.

....

....

....

....

....

....

January 16

Where you are right now
is God's place for you.

Live
and obey
and love
and believe

right there.

1 CORINTHIANS 7:17 MSG

January 17

Make dinner for a shut~in or a family in crisis.

Use disposable serving platters and include flowers.

....

....

....

....

....

....

January 18

In winter a tougher,
more resilient life is
firmly established.

Winter is necessary
for the tree
to survive
and flourish.

RICHARD J. FOSTER

....

....

....

....

....

January 19

Order pizza from a place
that offers two for one.
Deliver your extra pizza to a family in need.

....

....

....

....

....

....

January 20

Pray especially for rulers

and their governments
to rule well so we can be quietly
about our business of living simply.

1 TIMOTHY 2:2 MSG

....

....

....

....

....

....

January 21

Faith is taking the first step

even when you don't
see the whole staircase.

MARTIN LUTHER KING JR.

....

....

....

....

....

....

January 22

Give
sincere
compliments.

"Your hair looks great."
"I appreciate your follow-through."
"I wish I could clone you."
"I love the way your mind works."

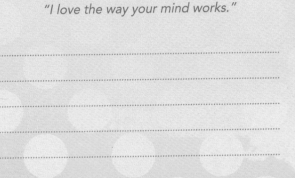

....

....

....

....

....

January 23

Accept a compliment graciously.

"Thanks. I needed to hear that today."

....

....

....

....

....

....

January 24

Taste
and see
that the LORD
is good.

PSALM 34:8 NIV

....

....

....

....

....

....

January 25

On a chilly night,

Warm the entire family's jammies in the dryer.

....

....

....

....

....

....

January 26

Say "yes!"

to more questions,
experiences,
and promptings
from God.

....
....
....
....
....
....

January 27

Be nice
to phone
solicitors.

You don't have to buy what they're selling,
but they're just doing their job and the
call is probably no fun for them either.

January 28

Be still,
and know
that
I am God.

PSALM 46:10 KJV

January 29

Preach less and
Practice
more.

....

....

....

....

....

....

January 30

Joy comes when
we catch
the rhythms of His heart.
Peace comes when we

Live in
harmony

with those rhythms.

KEN GIRE

....

....

....

....

....

....

January 31

Let someone else put in the last piece of a jigsaw puzzle.

(For fun, hide the last piece and select
a worthy person. Exclude yourself.)

....

....

....

....

....

....

February 1

Come to me,
all you who are weary and burdened,
and I will
give you rest.

MATTHEW 11:28 NIV

....

....

....

....

....

February 2

Compose a haiku.
Just seventeen syllables.
No need for rhyming.

....

....

....

....

....

....

February 3

Cuddle
newborns.

The first year of life
they will learn (or not learn)
the two most important
things in life: How to love.
How to be loved.

....

....

....

....

....

February 4

Don't
be afraid....
Remember the Lord,
who is great
and awesome.

NEHEMIAH 4:14 NIV

February 5

If there's no
line behind you,
go ahead and

Chat up
the cashier.

"So how are you today?"

....

....

....

....

....

....

February 6

Reflect
God's love.

Read 1 Peter 3:15–16.

When someone asks why you're
always so cheerful, tell them.

....

....

....

....

....

....

February 7

Relinquish the remote.

....

....

....

....

....

....

February 8

Don't take
yourself
too seriously~

take God seriously.

MICAH 6:8 MSG

....

....

....

....

....

....

February 9

Offer to babysit

for a young couple
or single parent.

....

....

....

....

....

February 10

Little deeds
of kindness,
little words
of love,
help to make
earth happy
Like the heaven above.

JULIA FLETCHER CARNEY

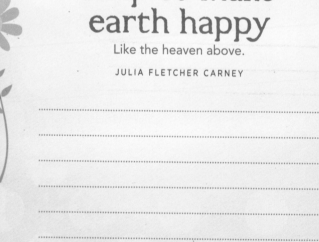

February 11

Pray for
the most
important
person
in your life.

....

....

....

....

....

February 12

Whatever you are, be a good one.

ABRAHAM LINCOLN

....

....

....

....

....

....

February 13

Sign your correspondence to your sweetie with exclamation points

and other fun symbols (!♥☺♫!).

....

....

....

....

....

....

February 14

Love extravagantly.

1 CORINTHIANS 13:13 MSG

....

....

....

....

....

....

February 15

You're blessed if you can

Laugh
at yourself,

for you will never cease to be amused.

....

....

....

....

....

....

February 16

Love the LORD your God with all your heart,

all your soul, and all your strength.

DEUTERONOMY 6:5 NLT

February 17

Mail a thank~you note

for an everyday
mundane gesture
that typically goes unnoticed.
Use a stamp!

....

....

....

....

....

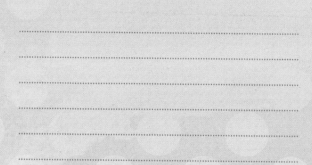

February 18

The ability to
Share
someone's
grief
is a gift from God.

JANETTE OKE

....

....

....

....

....

February 19

Thank your mom and dad.

You can never do that too often.

....

....

....

....

....

....

February 20

Guard
your heart,

for everything you do flows from it.

PROVERBS 4:23 NIV

....

....

....

....

....

February 21

Instead of a suggestion box,
get permission to
Put up a
prayer request
box
where you work,
play, worship, or dine.

....

....

....

....

....

....

February 22

Three words:
Share home~baked goods.

(Or is that four words?)

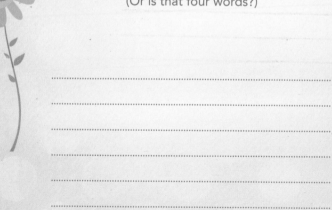

February 23

When you leave a voice mail,
repeat your phone number twice to

Make life
easier for the
other person

jotting down your message.

·····
·····
·····
·····
·····

February 24

Wait for the LORD;
be strong and let your
heart take courage.

PSALM 27:14 NASB

....

....

....

....

....

....

February 25

Listen...
to some old records.

Tell...
some old stories.

Watch...
some old TV shows.

....

....

....

....

....

February 26

Be willing to learn.

Everyone you meet knows
something you don't know.

....

....

....

....

....

February 27

Slip into the back of an open-door meeting for your community, church, school, or local government. If you're really brave,

When they ask for volunteers, raise your hand.

Be joyful in hope.

ROMANS 12:12 NIV

....

....

....

....

....

....

February 29

Return
borrowed
items
in original
condition

or better. If it's a car, return it washed,
vacuumed, and with a full gas tank.

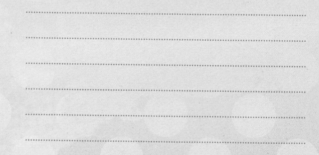

March 1

This month or another month with 31 days (January, May, July, August, October, or December)

Read one chapter from the book of Proverbs

per day.

....

....

....

....

....

....

March 2

Dress in the wardrobe God picked out for you:

compassion, kindness, humility,
quiet strength, discipline.

COLOSSIANS 3:12 MSG

March 3

Toss a
squishy ball
in the air

until someone signals you
to throw it their way. It never takes
more than 2¼ minutes. *Try it.*

....

....

....

....

....

March 4

Do a small good deed.

It's better than the
grandest intention.

....

....

....

....

....

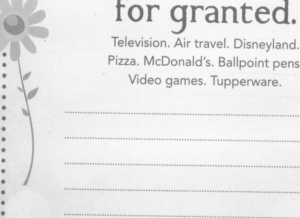

March 5

Ask someone over eighty about

the first time they experienced

stuff you take for granted.

Television. Air travel. Disneyland.
Pizza. McDonald's. Ballpoint pens.
Video games. Tupperware.

....

....

....

....

....

....

March 6

Seek
the LORD
your God

and you will find Him.

DEUTERONOMY 4:29 NKJV

March 7

Adjust your stride to arrive at a
doorway just in time to

Hold the
door open
for a group
of people.

....

....

....

....

....

....

March 8

Give credit where credit is due.

(Say "we" more than "I.")

....

....

....

....

....

....

March 9

Get a friend to talk about their hopes and dreams.

(Is there anything you can do to help them come true?)

....

....

....

....

....

....

March 10

Pray for absolutely everything,

ranging from small to large.

MARK 11:24 MSG

....

....

....

....

....

....

March 11

Remember that you are needed.

There is at least one important
work to be done that will not
be done unless you do it.

CHARLES L. ALLEN

March 12

Do something nice in secret.

(Keep it between you and God.)

....

....

....

....

....

....

March 13

Say
thank you
to the fast-food counter person
before they say it to you.

....

....

....

....

....

....

March 14

But those who trust
in the LORD WILL

Find new
strength.

They will soar high on wings like eagles.

ISAIAH 40:31 NLT

....

....

....

....

....

....

March 15

Cut
way, way,
way back
on sarcasm.

*"Even though it's so
endearing and uplifting!"*

....

....

....

....

....

March 16

Follow the recycling rules.

No cheesy pizza boxes.
Staples removed. No light bulbs.
Bottle caps off. Jars rinsed.
Consider the person doing the
sorting at the other end.

....

....

....

....

....

....

March 17

May you
Always remember when the shadows fall: you do not walk alone.

IRISH PROVERB

....

....

....

....

....

....

March 18

Be compassionate and loyal in your love.

MICAH 6:8 MSG

....

....

....

....

....

....

March 19

Memorize
a psalm.

A good place to start is with
chapter 1, 19, 23, 127, or 128.

....

....

....

....

....

....

March 20

Be a shock absorber.

Help a friend take the lumps and
bumps on the road of life.

FRANK TYGER, ADAPTED

....

....

....

....

....

....

March 21

Lend a smile
(and a helping hand)
to harried parents

in the airport. Just look around;
they're everywhere.

....

....

....

....

....

....

March 22

Give, and it will be given to you....

The measure you give will be the
measure you get back.

LUKE 6:38 NRSV

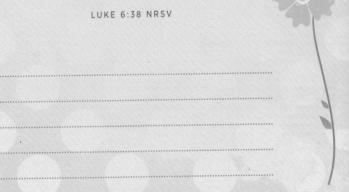

....

....

....

....

....

....

March 23

Teach a four-year-old to

Play rock/ paper/ scissors.

....

....

....

....

....

....

March 24

Have a
big enough
objective,

something which catches your imagination
and lays hold of your allegiance.

J. I. PACKER

....

....

....

....

....

....

March 25

Donate your old sports gear

to a boys' club or youth home.

....

....

....

....

....

....

March 26

See how great he is—

infinite, greater than anything you
could ever imagine or figure out!

JOB 36:26 MSG

....
....
....
....
....
....

March 27

Leave a
30 percent
tip

once in a while. (Or more!)

....

....

....

....

....

....

March 28

Do not forget the joy of Christ risen.

MOTHER TERESA

March 29

Prepare your family's favorite meal.

From scratch.

....

....

....

....

....

....

March 30

Let everything you say be good and helpful,

so that your words will be an encouragement
to those who hear them.

EPHESIANS 4:29 NLT

....

....

....

....

....

....

Stay in the left lane at stoplights

where there are two lanes, so cars
behind you can turn right on red.

....

....

....

....

....

....

April 1

When a toddler peeks over
the back of the booth,

Make your
silliest face.

....

....

....

....

....

....

April 2

Forgive
that one
person

you just haven't been able to.
Read Colossians 3:12–13.
Tell him or her you're
hoping for a fresh start.

....

....

....

....

....

April 3

In God's great mercy

He has caused us to be born again into a living hope,

because Jesus Christ rose from the dead.

1 PETER 1:3 NCV

April 4

Decorate the room of an older relative
with family photos, newspaper clippings,
etc., to spark conversations and

Affirm the life and contributions of the elderly.

April 5

Be accepting.

When you remember how hard
it is to change yourself, then you
begin to understand what little chance
you have of changing others.

....

....

....

....

....

....

April 6

Practice
saying
"Hey, need a
hand with that?"
(Say it out loud seven times right now
and then use your newfound skill!)

....

....

....

....

....

April 7

On the evening of that first
day of the week, when the disciples
were together...Jesus came and
stood among them and said,

"Peace be
with you!"

JOHN 20:19 NIV

....
....
....
....
....
....

April 8

Keep a small box of birthday candles in
your desk, cabinet, or purse. If someone
laments about turning a year older,

Create
an instant
celebration!

....

....

....

....

....

....

April 9

See the
promise of
resurrection
in every
leaf of
springtime.

....

....

....

....

....

April 10

Go out of your way to

Make the new person feel welcome

at school, work,
church, the gym,
your small group,
your social club, etc.

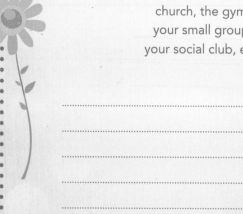

....

....

....

....

....

April 11

Do not let your heart be troubled;

believe in God, believe also in Me.

JOHN 14:1 NASB

April 12

Ask for help.

(*Too* many of us try to do *too* much on our own.)

....
....
....
....
....
....

April 13

Love the Lord your God with all your heart

and with all your soul
and with all your mind.

MATTHEW 22:37 NIV

....
....
....
....
....
....

April 14

On a rainy day,

Toss your neighbor's newspaper onto the porch.

....

....

....

....

....

....

April 15

Let us not grow weary in doing what is right,

for we will reap at harvest time,
if we do not give up.

GALATIANS 6:9 NRSV

April 16

Be a traffic angel.

Let
the other
car merge.

April 17

When other drivers let you merge,

Give a thank~you wave.

April 18

You make a living by
what you get, but you

Make a
life by
what
you give.

WINSTON CHURCHILL

....

....

....

....

....

....

April 19

Sing
and
give
praise.

PSALM 57:7 KJV

....

....

....

....

....

....

April 20

Offer your old golf clubs

or tennis racquet or hockey
stick or baseball glove

to a young neighbor.

(Misery loves company.)

....

....

....

....

....

April 21

Build a compost pile

and offer to take your
neighbor's yard waste.

....

....

....

....

....

April 22

Sign up to be
an organ donor.

Encourage the rest of your family
to be organ donors.

April 23

Look at the birds,

free and unfettered…careless
in the care of God. And

you count
far more to him
than birds.

MATTHEW 6:26 MSG

April 24

Give a basket of childproofing safety devices

to new parents. Cabinet locks. Outlet covers. First-aid kit. Syrup of Ipecac. Corner guards. TV straps. Toilet-seat locks.

....

....

....

....

....

....

April 25

Instead of judging,

Assume the best of everyone.

....
....
....
....

....

....

April 26

Carry an oversized umbrella
so you have room
to keep a stranger dry.

April 27

Let God transform you into a new person

by changing the way you think.

ROMANS 12:2 NLT

....

....

....

....

....

....

April 28

Organize a community garden.

Or participate in an existing garden.
Share your abundance.

....

....

....

....

....

....

April 29

Create an automatic signature
for your e-mails and

Share an
uplifting
quote

or one of the Scripture
verses in this book.

....
....
....
....
....
....

My life is God's prayer.

PSALM 42:8 MSG

May 1

Celebrate
May Day.

Leave a small
May Basket or bouquet
on your neighbors'
front porch.

....

....

....

....

....

....

May 2

In a conversation,

Really
listen.

Don't just wait for your
own opportunity to talk.

....

....

....

....

....

May 3

Thank God for His gifts.

Even if they aren't the ones you asked for.

May 4

Hire the local person.

Instead of calling the big firm with
the toll-free number, find a plumber,
electrician, cleaning lady, or tradesperson
who lives right in your hometown.

May 5

Don't worry about anything; instead, pray about everything.

Tell God what you need, and thank
him for all he has done.

PHILIPPIANS 4:6 NLT

....

....

....

....

....

....

May 6

Find a
new way
to worship
God today.

....
....
....
....
....
....

May 7

Every day is a clean
new page from
God for us to

Start
again.

....

....

....

....

....

....

May 8

Seize
the
moment.

Listen to crickets. Watch a hummingbird.
Smell the lilacs. Taste a strawberry.
Feel the grass with your bare feet.

....

....

....

....

....

May 9

Be easy
on people;

you'll find life a lot easier.

LUKE 6:37 MSG

May 10

Join the neighborhood watch.

Or start one.

May 11

Chaperone
a
field trip

for your local school or park district.

....

....

....

....

....

....

May 12

Call your mom

and tell her you love her.

···
···
···
···
···
···

May 13

Trust in the LORD with all your heart

and lean not on your own understanding.

PROVERBS 3:5 NIV

May 14

Take inventory of your unusual tools—

post-hole digger, wheelbarrow,
extension ladder, tile saw, power washer,
wallpaper steamer, appliance dolly—
and start a tool-lending library.

....

....

....

....

....

....

May 15

When your do-it-yourself
neighbor comes to
borrow a tool, offer to

Lend
a hand
as well.

....

....

....

....

....

....

May 16

Sing like there's nobody listening.

WILLIAM W. PURKEY

May 17

Be strong and courageous!

Do not be afraid.... The LORD your
God will personally go ahead of you.
He will neither fail you nor abandon you.

DEUTERONOMY 31:6 NLT

....

....

....

....

....

....

May 18

In a supermarket parking lot,
Grab the empty shopping cart
from someone leaving.

May 19

Speak words that are both
true and kind to someone who
needs to hear them. They can
Change
the world.

....

....

....

....

....

May 20

Reach out to your siblings.

At any age, they are the surest link
to your past and your future.

....

....

....

....

....

....

May 21

Learn to know God's will for you,

which is good and pleasing and perfect.

which is good and

ROMANS 12:2 NLT

....

....

....

....

....

....

May 22

Sit in an empty church and

Ask God to give you a specific, strategic plan

for your next season of life. He will.
(Actually, this works anywhere.)

....

....

....

....

....

....

May 23

Ride less and
Walk more

....

....

....

....

....

....

May 24

Plant
oodles of
flowers
on the side of the house
that you don't see very often but
your neighbor sees every day.

....

....

....

....

....

....

May 25

Take your everyday, ordinary life... and place it before God

as an offering. Embracing what God does for
you is the best thing you can do for him.

ROMANS 12:1 MSG

....

....

....

....

....

....

May 26

Show appreciation to a favorite teacher.

Consider a restaurant gift card instead of another apple-themed knickknack or wall hanging.

....

....

....

....

....

....

May 27

To God,
your country,
and your
friends
be true.

May 28

Bake some cookies
for your local firehouse.

....

....

....

....

....

....

May 29

Make the most of every opportunity.

COLOSSIANS 4:5 NIV

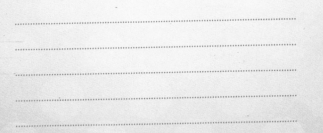

May 30

You are rich when
you choose to

Be content
with what
you have.

....

....

....

....

....

....

May 31

Stop by a VA hospital

or nursing home. At the front desk ask, *"Is there anyone who could use a visitor today?"*

....

....

....

....

....

....

June 1

Be
amazed

when a child brings you a bug,
dandelion, or shiny rock.

....

....

....

....

....

....

June 2

Why, my soul,
are you downcast?
Why so disturbed within me?

Put
your hope
in God.

PSALM 42: 5 NIV

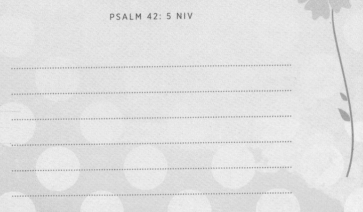

....

....

....

....

....

....

June 3

Share
sunscreen.

....

....

....

....

....

....

June 4

Turn strangers into friends.

Organize a neighborhood block party.

....

....

....

....

....

June 5

Seek first His kingdom and His righteousness,

and all these things will be added to you.

MATTHEW 6:33 NASB

....

....

....

....

....

....

June 6

Never, never, never quit.

WINSTON CHURCHILL

....
....
....
....
....
....

June 7

Give generously.

Read Malachi 3:10, Proverbs 11:25 and Luke 6:38. Trust you will be rewarded because you can't outgive God.

....

....

....

....

....

....

June 8

Tell your best friend how much she/he means to you.

"I don't know what I'd do without you."

....

....

....

....

....

June 9

Is someone you
care about facing chemo?

Throw a
bring~a~hat
party.

Even better, throw a
shave-your-head party.

....
....
....
....
....
....

June 10

Be what you were made to be,

without comparing yourself with others, or trying to be something you aren't.

ROMANS 12:6 MSG, ADAPTED

....

....

....

....

....

....

June 11

Support budding entrepreneurs.
Stop at every neighborhood lemonade stand.

....

....

....

....

....

....

June 12

Drive
ten miles
per hour
under the
speed limit
in kid-filled neighborhoods.

....

....

....

....

....

June 13

Recognize
that God
has a purpose
for your life
and no one else can take your place.

....
....
....
....
....
....

June 14

Show honor to your country's flag.

June 15

Tell
your dad
he's important
to you.

June 16

Never miss a local parade.

Stand on the curb.
March. Drive a convertible.
Roller skate. Unicycle.
Clean up afterward.

June 17

Ask an expert to teach you something new.

Juggling. Origami. Throwing a curve
ball. Knitting. Chess. Gardening.
Making pies from scratch.

....

....

....

....

....

....

June 18

Praise God....

Praise him under the open skies.

PSALM 150:1 MSG

June 19

Don't just swerve around it.

Stop your car and put the trash can back on the curb.

....

....

....

....

....

June 20

Bring
sunshine
into the
life of
someone else

and you'll be warmed by it yourself.

....

....

....

....

....

....

June 21

Renew your wedding vows.

Read 1 Corinthians 13:4–13.
Tell your spouse your love grows
stronger every day.

....
....
....
....
....
....

June 22

Live as children of light.

EPHESIANS 5:8 NIV

June 23

Teach a bunch of grade~school kids favorite outdoor games

from your youth. Hopscotch. Four Square. Kick the Can. Freeze Tag. Spud. Red Rover. Buck-Buck. Capture the Flag.

....

....

....

....

....

....

June 24

Do not forget little kindnesses,

and do not remember small faults.

CHINESE PROVERB

....

....

....

....

....

June 25

Feed the ducks.

Bring extra bread
or crackers for
other fowl fans.

....

....

....

....

....

....

June 26

Sing to the LORD a new song.

PSALM 96:1 NASB

....

....

....

....

....

....

June 27

Sit on a
park bench
and
blow bubbles.

....

....

....

....

....

June 28

Build bridges

instead of walls.

June 29

When your kid's
team is behind,

Pass around
a bag of
Tootsie Roll Pops.

Call them "Rally Pops."
Works every time!

....

....

....

....

....

....

June 30

Follow God's example

...as dearly loved children

EPHESIANS 5:1 NIV

....
....
....
....
....
....

July 1

On your next trip to the beach,
lake, river, or ocean,
bring a sturdy trash bag and

Clean up the shoreline

between bodysurfing
and sunbathing.

....

....

....

....

....

July 2

When life becomes all snarled up,

Hand everything to God and let Him untie the knots.

July 3

When your local supermarket has a
"buy-one-get-one-free" sale,

Buy two of a bunch of things and give away the "free" stuff.

....

....

....

....

....

....

July 4

Stand by your country, and celebrate your freedom.

....
....
....
....
....
....

July 5

Celebrate God all day, every day.

I mean, *revel* in him!

PHILIPPIANS 4:4 MSG

July 6

Get involved with the Special Olympics.

Volunteer. Donate. Or just show
up and cheer in the stands.
(It's unbelievably rewarding.)

July 7

Remember that God is in charge of your day~

not you.

CHARLES R. SWINDOLL, ADAPTED

....

....

....

....

....

....

July 8

Ask,
and it will
be given
to you.

LUKE 11:9 NKJV

....

....

....

....

....

....

July 9

Caught in a summer downpour?
Don't run.
Walk. Smile.
Laugh.
Be soggy.
(It's just water.)

July 10

Wherever you are, be *all there.*

Live to the hilt every situation you
believe to be the will of God.

JIM ELLIOT

....

....

....

....

....

....

July 11

Take a kid to a
professional baseball game.

Eat hot dogs
and
Cracker Jack

instead of buying a foam finger or
pennant. The ticket stub and the memories
are the more valuable souvenirs.

....

....

....

....

....

July 12

Even if you live a long time, don't
take a single day for granted.

Take delight
in each
light~filled
hour.

ECCLESIASTES 11:7-8 MSG

....

....

....

....

....

....

July 13

Pray your frustrations away.

The dog that barks all night.
The gossipmonger at work.
The pothole you hit twice a day.
The keys you lost two weeks ago.

....

....

....

....

....

July 14

Take courage!

Count your blessings,

not your losses.

BARBARA JOHNSON

July 15

Remember friends' anniversaries.

Not just wedding anniversaries. The death of a loved one. The difficult move to a new city. The deployment of a son or daughter. A year since the layoff. (They're already silently marking the date; your remembrance will mean so much.)

....

....

....

....

....

....

July 16

Carry
each
other's
burdens,

and in this way you will
fulfill the law of Christ.

GALATIANS 6:2 NIV

July 17

Buy fresh
produce
at a farmer's
market

directly from the people who grow it.

July 18

Be there for someone.
Show real interest and concern.

....

....

....

....

....

....

July 19

Accomplish humble tasks

as though they were great and noble..

HELEN KELLER

....

....

....

....

....

....

July 20

Encourage one another daily,

as long as it is called "Today."

HEBREWS 3:13 NIV

July 21

Play the guitar on your front porch.

(During "reasonable" hours only.)

July 22

Give
without
remembering

and take without forgetting.

ELIZABETH BIBESCO

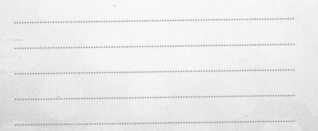

July 23

Give someone a second chance.

....
....
....
....
....
....

July 24

Consider the lilies of the field...
if God so clothes the grass of the field...
will He not much more clothe you?

MATTHEW 6:28-30 NKJV

....

....

....

....

....

....

July 25

Write
"I ♥ U"
on a
sticky note

and leave it on the bathroom mirror of
someone who needs that reminder.

....

....

....

....

....

....

July 26

Although you cannot
change the direction
of the wind, you can
Adjust
your
sails.

....

....

....

....

....

....

July 27

Pet the
pooch
in the park.

(Ask the owner first.)

....

....

....

....

....

....

July 28

If you need wisdom, ask our generous God,

and he will give it to you.

JAMES 1:5 NLT

July 29

Hold a garage sale.

Instead of haggling over prices, let
buyers set their own prices.

Donate all proceeds to a favorite charity.

....

....

....

....

....

....

July 30

Grow as beautiful as God meant you to be

when He thought of you first.

GEORGE MACDONALD

....

....

....

....

....

....

July 31

Want to do something really beautiful?

Toss all
your beauty
magazines.

....

....

....

....

....

....

August 1

Let's not just
talk about love; let's
Practice
real love.

1 JOHN 3:18 MSG

....
....
....
....
....
....

August 2

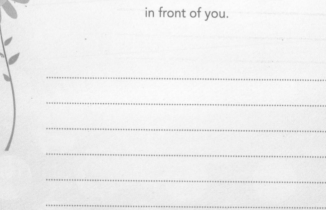

Instead of a curse,

Offer a prayer for the driver who swerves

in front of you.

....

....

....

....

....

....

August 3

Thou shalt

Obey the "10 items or less" sign.

Thou shalt not glare at those who don't.

August 4

Share
bug
spray.

....

....

....

....

....

....

August 5

Love
one
another.

1 PETER 3:8 NIV

....

....

....

....

....

....

August 6

Bring extra water

to outdoor summer events.
Toss a bottle to a thirsty stranger.

....

....

....

....

....

....

August 7

Tweet or

Brag about the awesomeness of your spouse, kid, friend, or coworker.

....

....

....

....

....

....

August 8

Tweet or
Brag about the awesomeness of your neighborhood, town, church, or country.

....

....

....

....

....

....

August 9

Cast your cares on the LORD

and he will sustain you.

PSALM 55:22 NIV

....

....

....

....

....

....

August 10

Offer to water your neighbors' plants

and get their mail, even if they have been bragging about their dream vacation and you're stuck at home.

....

....

....

....

....

August 11

If you find yourself
dominating a conversation,
Ask a question
and listen
to the answer.

....

....

....

....

....

....

August 12

On the way home from a restaurant,

Personally deliver a special treat

to a casual acquaintance who
doesn't get out much.

....

....

....

....

....

....

August 13

Take my yoke

upon you and learn from me, for I
am gentle and humble in heart,

and you will
find rest for
your souls.

MATTHEW 11:29 NIV

August 14

If someone mentions
weekend plans
involving yard work, painting,
deck building, or fence repair...

Volunteer
your help

before they ask!

August 15

Things turn out best
for the people who
Make the best of the way things turn out.

ART LINKLETTER

August 16

When your kids move out, let them take something special.

Furniture. Dishes. Small appliances.
Framed photos. Every time they
see it, they'll think of home.

....
....
....
....
....
....

August 17

Love each other with
genuine affection, and

Take delight
in honoring
each other.

ROMANS 12:10 NLT

....

....

....

....

....

....

August 18

Pick your favorite age group
(babies, toddlers, elementary,
middle, high school, college,
singles, seniors) and

Get
involved

with that age at your church.
Commit to once a week for one year.

....
....
....
....
....
....

Speak kind words and you will hear kind echoes.

MOTHER TERESA

....

....

....

....

....

August 20

Picnic.

Prepare a gourmet meal
and hike into a park.
Or grab an inexpensive
box lunch and eat it on a
blanket in your yard.

....

....

....

....

....

....

August 21

Keep
a firm grip
on the
promises

that keep us going. He always keeps his word.

HEBREWS 10:23 MSG

August 22

Find an excuse to

Spend ten minutes with an elderly neighbor.

Ask their advice. Have them
recommend a plumber.
Compliment their roses. Pet their dog.

....

....

....

....

....

....

August 23

Train yourself not to worry.

Worry never fixes anything.

MARY HEMINGWAY

....

....

....

....

....

....

August 24

Sign up for an excursion with your local
park district, church group, community
outreach, or veteran's group.

Invite a friend who doesn't get out much to join you.

....

....

....

....

....

....

August 25

Take a Sunday drive.

Like in the old days.

....

....

....

....

....

....

August 26

May...God...fill you up
with joy, fill you up with peace,
so that your believing lives...will

Brim over
with hope!

ROMANS 15:13 MSG

....

....

....

....

....

....

August 27

Make time to exercise.

Especially if you are under stress
and don't have enough time.

August 28

Don't try to be cool.

**As a matter of fact,
try to be uncool.**

....
....
....
....
....
....

August 29

Let your conversation be always full of grace

...so that you may know how
to answer everyone.

COLOSSIANS 4:6 NIV

August 30

After dinner,
Stroll
around
the block
with someone you love.

....

....

....

....

....

August 31

Use the Internet to
Track down a favorite teacher from years ago.
Call and say,
"You made a difference in my life."

....

....

....

....

....

....

September 1

Make eye contact

with a homeless person
or someone you don't know.
Say, *"Hi! How are you?"*

....

....

....

....

....

September 2

Enjoy the fruits of your labor,

for these are gifts from God.

ECCLESIASTES 3:13 NLT, ADAPTED

September 3

Write encouraging Scripture verses on index cards.

Tuck them into books, calendars, magazines, file folders, and drawers for you—and others—to discover later.

....

....

....

....

....

....

September 4

Learn to say hello in at least ten languages.

Hola. Bonjour. Shalom. Guten tag. Konnichiwa.
Zdravstvuyte. Jambo. Xin chao. Aloha.

....

....

....

....

....

....

September 5

Go to a Friday night high school football game

or other sporting event.
Cheer for the home team.

....

....

....

....

....

....

September 6

Commit
to the LORD
whatever
you do,

and he will establish your plans.

PROVERBS 16:3 NIV

September 7

Pick up after yourself.

And if you have a dog,
pick up after your pooch—
in yards, parks, and parkways.

September 8

Put an extra cookie in a separate plastic bag

in your kid's lunch box.
Include a note that says, *"Give this to
a friend sitting across the table."*

September 9

At the tollbooth, coffee shop,
or fast-food window,

Pay for
the person
behind you.

....

....

....

....

....

September 10

Hope
unswervingly.

1 CORINTHIANS 13:13 MSG

....

....

....

....

....

....

September 11

Americans are asking,
"What is expected of us?"…

Live your
lives
and hug
your children.

GEORGE W. BUSH

....

....

....

....

....

....

September 12

Memorize
a poem

and recite it to a friend later.

....

....

....

....

....

....

September 13

Join the neighborhood kids in a game

of touch football, soccer, or basketball.
(If teams are already even, offer to be
scorekeeper or cheerleader for both sides.)

....
....
....
....
....
....

September 14

Rejoice and be glad in today.

PSALM 118:24 NKJV, ADAPTED

September 15

What higher and
more compelling goal
can there be than to

Know God.

J. I. PACKER

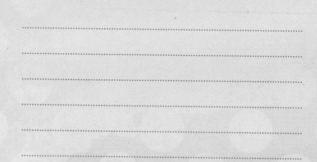

September 16

Pull into the car wash

sponsored by the high school
sports boosters.
Even if your car isn't dirty.

....

....

....

....

....

....

September 17

Be a support to new moms

who don't have a ton of family support.
Especially single moms, military wives,
and underemployed families.

....

....

....

....

....

....

September 18

Love your neighbor as yourself.

MATTHEW 22:39 NIV

....

....

....

....

....

....

September 19

Start a Bible study

at your place of work
or public school.
(Yes, it's legal!)

....

....

....

....

....

....

September 20

Give yourself permission to be happy.

Give *someone else*
permission to be happy.

....

....

....

....

....

....

September 21

In a profound way,
our intentionality is a
key ingredient determining
whether we

Notice God everywhere.

ELIZABETH DREYER

....

....

....

....

....

....

September 22

Cast all your anxiety on him

because he cares for you.

1 PETER 5:7 NIV

....

....

....

....

....

....

September 23

Ask for the pretty stamps

at the post office. Use them
on bills, thank-you notes, and
messages from a secret admirer.

....

....

....

....

....

September 24

Take your spouse on a date.

Or do something special
with a close friend.

....

....

....

....

....

....

September 25

Say "thanks" or "hi"

to people who keep the
world turning. Busboys.
Baggers. Custodians. Bus drivers.
Ticket takers. Food servers.
Mail carriers.

....

....

....

....

....

....

September 26

Love God...
walk in
his ways...

so that you will live, really live,
live exuberantly, blessed by God.

DEUTERONOMY 30:16 MSG

....

....

....

....

....

September 27

Work hard.

*Read Colossians 3:23
and 2 Thessalonians 3:10–12.*
Consider it a privilege
to use the skills and gifts
God has given you.

....

....

....

....

....

....

September 28

Take a nature walk and
Praise God for His creativity.

....

....

....

....

....

....

September 29

Instead of just saying,
"Great sermon, Pastor,"

Compliment
specifics

that touched your mind and heart.

....

....

....

....

....

....

September 30

Steep
yourself in
God~reality,

God-initiative, God-provisions.
You'll find all your everyday
human concerns will be met.

LUKE 12:31 MSG

October 1

Organize
a sock or
mitten drive.

October 2

Do a two-for-one:
Invite someone to do something beautiful with you.

....

....

....

....

....

October 3

Throw a
sweet party!

(Literally.) Make your own ice cream.
Or taffy. Or cotton candy.
Or S'mores on a campfire.

....

....

....

....

....

....

October 4

Be strong in the Lord and in his mighty power.

EPHESIANS 6:10 NIV

....

....

....

....

....

October 5

Take a class at a community
education program
or local college. Your goal:

Make at
least one
new friend.

....

....

....

....

....

....

October 6

Have a positive spirit.

Make it contagious—
transmit it to someone else.

ANNE FRANK

....

....

....

....

....

....

October 7

With construction paper,
crayons, glitter,
scissors, and glue,

Make a
greeting card.

Then give it to someone special.

October 8

Knock, and it will be opened to you.

LUKE 11:9 NKJV

October 9

Two words:
Prison
ministry.

....

....

....

....

....

....

October 10

Experience God in the breathless wonder

and startling beauty
that is all around you.

WENDY MOORE

October 11

Go to the effort. Invest the time.
Write the letter. Make the apology.
Take the trip. Purchase the gift.

Do it.
The seized
opportunity
renders joy.

MAX LUCADO

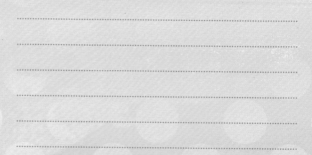

October 12

Be kind
to one
another,
tender~hearted,

forgiving each other, just as God in
Christ also has forgiven you.

EPHESIANS 4:32 NASB

....

....

....

....

....

October 13

Save newspaper clippings

for your neighbor when their kid's name is mentioned. (Only for *accomplishments*, not in the police report.)

....

....

....

....

....

....

October 14

Donate
blood.

October 15

Rake your neighbor's leaves,

or mow your neighbor's lawn,
trim your neighbor's hedges,
weed your neighbor's garden,
curb your neighbor's trash.

....

....

....

....

....

....

October 16

Love from the center of who you are;

don't fake it.

ROMANS 12:9 MSG

....

....

....

....

....

....

October 17

Organize a scavenger hunt.

....

....

....

....

....

....

October 18

If you cannot do
something great today,
Do small
things
in a
great way.

....

....

....

....

....

October 19

Don't just read a book to a child,
Use silly character voices when you read.

....

....

....

....

....

....

October 20

Pray
every way
you
know how,
for everyone you know.

1 TIMOTHY 2:1 MSG

October 21

Scan Grandma's handwritten
recipe cards and

Create an ever~expanding web~based family cookbook

for future generations.

....

....

....

....

....

....

October 22

Be an instrument of God's peace.

ST. FRANCIS OF ASSISI, ADAPTED

....

....

....

....

....

October 23

On extreme weather days,

Meet your mail carrier at the mailbox with steaming cocoa

or ice water to go.
Or a fresh-baked oatmeal cookie!

....

....

....

....

....

....

October 24

Delight yourself in the LORD;

and He will give you
the desires of your heart.

PSALM 37:4 NASB

October 25

When you attend
a sporting event,

Cheer
great plays

by both teams.

....

....

....

....

....

....

October 26

Don't
over~cheer
when the other team makes an error.

....
....
....
....
....
....

October 27

Get
less
done,

but the right things.

JEAN FLEMING

October 28

Clothe yourself with love,

which binds us all together in perfect harmony.

COLOSSIANS 3:14 NLT, ADAPTED

....

....

....

....

....

....

October 29

Tackle
the pile of
mismatched
socks.

....

....

....

....

....

....

October 30

Remember, God is
already there, so

Don't fear
tomorrow.

....

....

....

....

....

October 31

At Halloween,

drop awesome treats into trick-or-treat
bags. But also include bookmarks or
tracts with uplifting messages to

counteract
the dark forces
of the day.

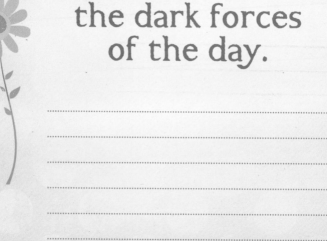

November 1

I've loved you the way
my Father has loved me.

Make
yourselves
at home
in my love.

JOHN 15:9 MSG

....

....

....

....

....

....

November 2

Pray
out loud

with your family.
Even in public.

....

....

....

....

....

....

November 3

Put your
gifts to
the best use
you can.

November 4

One vote can change a nation.

One life can make a difference.
That difference starts with you.

....

....

....

....

....

....

November 5

Trust in
Him at
all times.

PSALM 62:8 NASB

....

....

....

....

....

November 6

Offer to
Do a chore
for your dad
so he can
watch the game.

(You know it would make his week.)

....

....

....

....

....

....

November 7

Create space for others

on the subway, bus, or elevator.
Slide over. Grab the next pole.
Move away from the doors.
Keep your bags (and feet) out of the way.

....

....

....

....

....

....

November 8

Welcome the new neighbors with flowers and brownies.

Or maybe finally meet the longtime neighbors you've never talked with!

....

....

....

....

....

....

November 9

Trust
steadily
in God.

1 CORINTHIANS 13:13 MSG

....

....

....

....

....

November 10

Pick up
the
dinner tab

for new parents when you encounter
them at a restaurant.

....

....

....

....

....

....

November 11

Thank a veteran for his or her service.

....

....

....

....

....

....

November 12

Anonymously leave a bag of candy

for the person at work with the
candy dish on their desk.

....

....

....

....

....

....

November 13

Draw
near to
God

with a sincere heart
and with the full assurance
that faith brings.

HEBREWS 10:22 NIV

November 14

Downsize
your life.

A smaller house and
smaller cash flow may give you freedom
to do great and beautiful things.

....

....

....

....

....

....

November 15

Frown less and
Laugh
more.

....

....

....

....

....

....

November 16

After a night of
good conversation
with dinner guests,

Make a gift
of a book

that relates to your table talk.

....

....

....

....

....

November 17

Rejoice
always.

1 THESSALONIANS 5:16 NIV

November 18

Try seeing people through God's eyes.

(You may have to squint from time to time.)

November 19

It is only with gratitude that life becomes rich.

DIETRICH BONHOEFFER

....

....

....

....

....

....

November 20

Lay aside some important work to play with a child.

These small choices may affect lives eternally.

GLORIA GAITHER

....

....

....

....

....

November 21

Give thanks
to the LORD,
for he is good!

His faithful love endures forever.

PSALM 106:1 NLT

November 22

Make
a list of
ten people who
helped you

become who you are today. Thank half
of them before the sun goes down.

....

....

....

....

....

....

November 23

Get a bigger bucket.

The well of Providence
is deep. It's the buckets we
bring to it that are small.

MARY WEBB

....

....

....

....

....

....

November 24

Start a gratitude journal.

....

....

....

....

....

....

November 25

In everything give thanks.

1 THESSALONIANS 5:18 NKJV

November 26

Make your
love visible

through little acts of kindness, shared
activities, words of praise and thanks,
and willingness to get along.

EDWARD E. FORD

....
....
....
....
....
....

November 27

Savor little glimpses of God's goodness

and His majesty, thankful for the gift of them.

....

....

....

....

....

....

November 28

Around the meal table,

Count all the things you have that money can't buy.

....

....

....

....

....

....

November 29

O my soul, bless GOD,

Don't forget a single blessing!

PSALM 103:2 MSG

....

....

....

....

....

November 30

Give firm handshakes.

Add a smile and a *"Good to meet you!"*

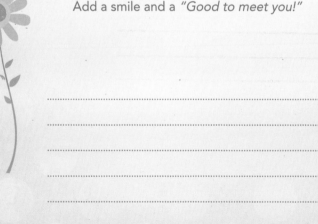

December 1

Wake the carol—sound the chime—

Welcome!
Merry
Christmas
time!

HELEN CHASE

....

....

....

....

....

December 2

Give your frequent flyer miles

to help a college student or soldier or missionary on furlough come home for Christmas.

December 3

Fix your thoughts on what is true,

and honorable, and right, and pure,
and lovely, and admirable.

PHILIPPIANS 4:8 NLT

December 4

Write a letter to your oldest living relative

Make it newsy, grateful, lighthearted.

....

....

....

....

....

....

December 5

Leave notes of encouragement in unexpected places.

Lunch boxes. Briefcases. Bathroom mirrors.
Pillows. Steering wheels. Laptops.

....

....

....

....

....

December 6

Let the day suffice,
with all its joys and failings,
its little triumphs and defeats....

Welcome
evening
as a time
of rest,

and let it slip away, losing nothing.

KATHLEEN NORRIS

....

....

....

....

....

....

December 7

Love each other as God has loved you.

JOHN 15:12 NIV, ADAPTED

....

....

....

....

....

....

December 8

Do your
own chore
without complaining.
Do someone
else's chore
without letting anyone know.

....
....
....
....
....
....

December 9

When you meet someone new, use their name three times

in that first conversation.

....

....

....

....

....

....

December 10

Be ten minutes early

for appointments.

December 11

Always be eager to practice hospitality.

ROMANS 12:13 NLT

....

....

....

....

....

....

December 12

Put a twenty in the Salvation Army kettle.

Or dig in your pocket pretending to look for loose change, but really drop in a gold coin! (Don't tell anyone!)

....

....

....

....

....

December 13

Let Christmas in its deepest magic possess your mind.

The Lord of Glory, "endless, eternal and unchangeable in His being, wisdom, power, and holiness," became…a baby.

JACK HAYFORD

December 14

For somehow, not only at Christmas,
but all the long year through,

The joy that you
give to others

is the joy that

comes back to you.

JOHN GREENLEAF WHITTIER

December 15

Give generously,

for your gifts will return to you later.

ECCLESIASTES 11:1 TLB

....

....

....

....

....

....

December 16

In a retail store or restaurant,

Tell the manager when you get exceptional service.

Good words trickle down and
are much appreciated.

....

....

....

....

....

....

December 17

Some gifts are big, others are small.

Gifts from the heart are the best gifts of all.

....

....

....

....

....

....

December 18

Carol
in your
neighborhood,
at a senior home,
or at a disability center.

December 19

Rejoice with those who rejoice.

ROMANS 12:15 NASB

December 20

At
Christmas,
play and make
good cheer,

for Christmas comes but once a year.

THOMAS TUSSER

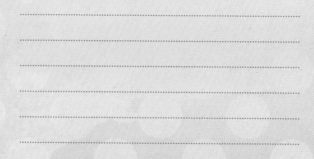

December 21

Life is filled with many gifts—unwrap the ribbons.

....

....

....

....

....

December 22

The best
thing to give

to your enemy is forgiveness;
to an opponent, tolerance;
to a friend, your heart;

to all people,
is charity.

LORD BALFOUR

....

....

....

....

....

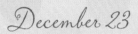

December 23

Glory to God in
highest heaven, and

Peace
on earth

to those with whom
God is pleased.

LUKE 2:14 NLT

December 24

At this special time of year:

Follow
the
children.

Hear the joy in their laughter.
See the love in their eyes.
Feel the hope in their hearts.

....

....

....

....

....

....

December 25

Come and behold Him,
born the King of angels!

O come
let us
adore Him,
Christ the Lord!

JOHN FRANCIS WADE

....

....

....

....

....

....

December 26

Save your Christmas cards,

pictures, and greetings. Select one per day and say a prayer for those friends or family members.

....

....

....

....

....

....

December 27

Live in complete harmony with each other.

ROMANS 15:5 NLT

December 28

Look on the new day as another
special gift from your Creator,
another golden opportunity...to

Complete what you were unable to finish yesterday.

OG MANDINO

....

....

....

....

....

....

December 29

Trust the past to the mercy of God,

the present to His love, and the
future to His providence.

AUGUSTINE

....

....

....

....

....

....

December 30

Look at the sunset and see the promise of a new dawn.

....

....

....

....

....

....

December 31

You get a fresh start, your slate's wiped clean.

PSALM 32:1 MSG

....

....

....

....

....

Ellie Claire™ Gift & Paper Corp.
Minneapolis, MN 55378
EllieClaire.com

Do Something Beautiful 365-Day Journal
© 2013 by Ellie Claire Gift & Paper Corp.

ISBN 978-1-60936-911-8

Scripture quotations are taken from The Holy Bible, King James Version (KJV). The Holy Bible, New International Version®, NIV®. Copyright © 1973, 1978, 1984, 2011 by Biblica, Inc.™ Used by permission of Zondervan. All rights reserved worldwide. The Holy Bible, New King James Version (NKJV). Copyright © 1997, 1990, 1985, 1983 by Thomas Nelson, Inc. The New American Standard Bible® (NASB), copyright © 1960, 1962, 1963, 1968, 1971, 1972, 1973, 1975, 1977, 1995 by The Lockman Foundation. Used by permission. The Holy Bible, New Living Translation (NLT), copyright 1996, 2004, 2007 by Tyndale House Foundation. Used by permission of Tyndale House Publishers, Inc., Carol Stream, Illinois 60188. *The Message* (MSG). Copyright © 1993, 1994, 1995, 1996, 2000, 2001, 2002 by Eugene Peterson. Used by permission of NavPress, Colorado Springs, CO. All rights reserved.

The forms of LORD and GOD in quotations from the Bible represent the Hebrew *Yahweh*, while Lord and God represent *Adonai*, in accordance with the Bible version used.

Many of the beautiful action items herein were compiled by best-selling author Jay Payleitner and culled from the inspired whimsy and brainstorming of a variety of talented characters including Sue Curran, Kenzie Curran, Emily Curran, Mary Kay Coleman, Katie Nelson, Rachel Payleitner, Randall Payleitner, Lindsay Payleitner, Alec Payleitner, Megan Payleitner, Max Payleitner, Isaac Payleitner, Stephanie Payleitner and Mark Payleitner. Others compiled by the editors of Ellie Claire. For more creative relationship-building ideas, visit jaypayleitner.com.

This project is represented by MacGregor Literary Inc., Hillsboro, Oregon.

Cover and interior design by Greg Jackson | ThinkPen Design.
Typesetting by Jeff Jansen | AestheticSoup.net

Printed in China.